Rabbit Chinese Horoscope 2025

By
IChingHunFùyǒu FengShuisu

Table of Contents

Introduce

The character of people born in the year of the Rabbit

People born in the Rabbit year are gentle and caring. You are also a good friend and condescending person, in addition to having a kind, sweet, and affectionate nature. I dislike making others unhappy. Rabbits appreciate beauty, are artistic, and have refined taste. Despite being loved by friends and family, Snakes remain pessimistic, fearful, conservative, and easily insecure. Making it someone who dislikes change.

People born this year are reserved, making it difficult to awaken the Snake's mood. In any case, he dislikes arguing and prefers a quiet life. Frequently timid or skeptical That is, Snakes frequently have to weigh the pros and cons before deciding what to do.

Strength:

Rabbit people are well-mannered people who are always loved by everyone.

Weaknesses:
Likes to be alone dislikes loud noises, is easily startled, and can be overly timid at times.

Love:
People born in this year are sensitive, gentle, fanciful, and less firm in their love. If you want to love someone born in the year of the Rabbit, you must be willing to endure some pain. Don't expect the bunnies to last. He or she has a weak heart. If someone comes to do good deeds with them, they are enthralled and can't take their eyes off them. People born this year are notoriously envious. Because if you love someone, you usually won't let anyone else take it away from you. People born in this year prefer to always create an atmosphere of new love. Couples born this year There is no boredom or emotionlessness. It also has a strong love mood.

Suitable Career:
People born in the Year of the Rabbit belong to the Wood element. Known occupations are thus primarily related to wood, such as tree

planting, landscaping, furniture making, wood trading, or work related to business trips related to telecommunications or work that requires extensive contact and negotiation with people, such as guides. Create a tour company, hire a DJ, and work in public relations. Department coordination, sales, creative, selling mobile phones or satellite dishes, and so on, including export business and dealing with foreigners. All of these occupations are appropriate for the Year of the Snake.

Year of the Rabbit (Earth) | (1939) & (1999)

"The Rabbit in the Wild" is a person born in the year of the Rabbit at the age of 86 years (1939) and 26 years (1999)

Overview

For senior horoscopes in this age group, this year the horoscope will have a comfortable life and will have enough money to spend. However, during the year, there will be the influence of bad stars that come in, causing unexpected current expenses to take money out of pocket. Therefore, when money flows in, you should save it for emergencies. The important thing this year is to let go of things and take care of your health consistently, both in terms of eating and living. Also, you should avoid being nosy about your children and grandchildren. Life at this age will be happy.

For young horoscopes, this year is another auspicious year with auspicious stars shining in the horoscope house, which will have a good effect on some horoscopes who will start their businesses or open their businesses. For those who work regularly, their careers will have a path of progress. Therefore, please prepare a plan and lay a foundation for the future. Always increase your skills and knowledge to keep up with events. This year, if the horoscope is planning to buy a house, buy a car, or plan to study abroad, all will have a good direction and will see progress because the preparation or starting work this year will receive smooth energy. But during the year, due to the appearance of the evil star "betrayal star" which in addition to affecting your emotions will make you feel irritated and easily irritated, seeing anything that seems to be unpleasant, and those who do not like you will easily cause arguments, you have a chance to meet bad friends, may be taken advantage of and used, and may encounter gossip and slander. Therefore, you should be careful. In addition, try to avoid going to indecent places that will bring disaster. As for traveling and working, be careful of accidents. During the unfavorable months, be careful of people secretly attacking you, and be careful of losing valuables. But in terms of love, it is bright and cheerful because auspicious stars are visiting the horoscope house, which will encourage those who are still single. This year, there will be a good time to meet your soulmate. For those who have a lover or partner, there will be understanding and a stronger relationship.

Career and Business

This year, your career is prosperous. If you work in a company or organization, this year you will have the opportunity to take on more responsibility at work. If you build and strengthen relationships in your organization well, this year you will likely be promoted. Therefore, please be diligent and take good care of your work and, ideally, you should learn from your seniors or those who are more senior. In addition, you should be interested in developing yourself in new skills related to your regular work or part-time job, which will benefit you in the future. Especially during the months when your work will have a direction of progress and prosperity, namely, the 12th Chinese month (January 5 – February 2), the 3rd Chinese month (April 4 – May 4), the 7th

Chinese month (August 7 – September 6), and the 9th Chinese month (October 8 – November 6). In addition, working together or investing with others, including investing in various areas during this period, will have a good direction. You can choose to invest and will have satisfactory returns. However, during this year, your horoscope encounters bad stars that harass you, causing you to often have conflicts with people in your organization. In particular, the months when your work will be hindered and have many obstacles are the 2nd Chinese month (5 March – 3 April), the 4th Chinese month (5 May – 4 June), the 5th Chinese month (5 June – 6 July), and the 8th Chinese month (7 September – 7 October) in which you should use moral principles as your guide. Do not use the method of responding in a way that if someone is harsh, you will be harsh back because in the end both parties will be severely hurt. In addition, you should always adhere to the principles of working with friendliness, kindness, and consideration for others. This will allow you to achieve sustainable progress.

Financial

In terms of financial luck, even though this year your income will be good, so you won't have to worry too much about struggling to find it, but you will encounter unexpected expenses more than usual. When you add, subtract, multiply, and divide, you will have almost no money left to save. Therefore, you should manage your income and expenses well from the beginning of the year. Always save and save money, especially during the months when your finances are low and unexpected expenses occur, such as the 2nd Chinese month (March 5 – April 3), the 4th Chinese month (May 5 – June 4), the 5th Chinese month (June 5 – July 6), and the 8th Chinese month (September 7 – October 7), in which you should not lend money to others or sign as a financial guarantee. Also, you should not invest in businesses that infringe copyright or are against the law. The months when your finances will flow smoothly are the 12th Chinese month (5 January – 2 February), the 3rd Chinese month (4 April – 4 May), the 7th Chinese month (7 August – 6 September), and the 9th Chinese month (8 October – 6 November).

Family

This year, your family will encounter an auspicious constellation sending auspicious energy into your home, which will lead to a patron. Even if there are conflicts, they will be resolved. There is also a chance that an auspicious event will occur. You may move into a new house or have more family members. However, you should be careful during the months when family members will easily have conflicts and arguments, which are the 2nd Chinese month (March 5 – April 3), the 4th Chinese month (May 5 – June 4), the 5th Chinese month (June 5 – July 6), and the 8th Chinese month (September 7 – October 7). In addition, you must be careful of your juniors causing trouble. Be careful of unexpected changes in events. Be careful of valuable property damage, loss, or theft. You must also be careful of injuries from accidents. As for your relatives, you should consider them carefully this year because the Huang Pui star (the betrayal star) is staring at you in your zodiac sign, which will result in conflicts. There may be gossip, backstabbing, or betrayal. Therefore, you should be careful if money is involved between your friends. Including speech, you should be careful with some words that you say without thinking but may hurt someone, who may come back to hurt you later.

Love

For senior horoscopes, this year, please do not be fussy or interfere with your children's and grandchildren's matters, and everyone in the house will respect and love you. For horoscopes around the age of 26, this year's love horoscope is good because the Ang Lueng star (red bird star) is visiting the horoscope house, so love matters will feel sweet. For those who are still single, you will be charming and attract the attention of the opposite sex. This year, there will be a chance to meet someone you like, and there will be an opportunity to continue a long-term relationship. For some couples, this year will be a good time to ask for love, as well as an auspicious date for engagement, marriage, or childbirth. However, you should be careful during the months when your love is quite fragile and conflicts can easily arise, such as the 2nd Chinese month (March 5 – April 3), the 4th Chinese month (May 5 – June 4), the 5th Chinese month (June 5 – July 6), and the 8th Chinese month (September 7 – October 7). You should avoid interfering in other people's family matters. Be careful that misunderstandings will cause arguments from small matters to big ones. You should also avoid visiting entertainment venues that secretly sell services, as you may catch an illness that will cause you trouble.

Health

Health for the elderly This year, be careful of old illnesses that may flare up or latent illnesses that threaten you. Therefore, you should get enough rest and not be stressed. When your mind is at ease, your physical health will be good. As for the health of young men and women, this year you should be careful of gastritis, intestinal inflammation, problems with the appendix, accumulated diseases caused by eating whatever you want, and food poisoning. The months that the elderly in both cycles should take close care of their health are the 2nd Chinese month (March 5 – April 3), the 4th Chinese month (May 5 – June 4), the 5th Chinese month (June 5 – July 6), and the 8th Chinese month (September 7 – October 7). You should be more careful, especially about the hygiene of your food and drink. You should also be careful of accidents while working and traveling.

Year of the Rabbit (Wood) | (1951) & (2011)
" The Rabbit on the Moon " is a person born in the year of the Rabbit at the age of 74 years (1951) and 14 years (2011)

Overview
For senior horoscopes, this year is another year that will receive auspicious power. During the year, you will have the opportunity to travel both domestically and internationally, traveling with close relatives, friends, or children. There will also be an opportunity to

join merit-making ceremonies. However, you should be careful about your health, see a doctor regularly as scheduled, and take your medication as prescribed, and this year you should find time to make merit to help reduce health calamities. You should also relax, not be stressed, and should not be too fussy with your children or grandchildren. In addition, you should be more careful about the dangers of water.

For horoscopes around the age of 14, because this age is full of energy and is seeking new things, it is easy to make mistakes. In addition, for both good and bad people in society outside the home and online, you must know how to say no sometimes, otherwise you will be led to try wrong things or go astray. This year, you will suffer and have dangers because of your friends. Therefore, you should be careful and try not to go to nightlife places. You must also be careful of children who do not wish you well, including various temptations that will cause you to lose concentration in studying. Therefore, please separate playtime and study time into discipline. You should also know how to control your temper. When you have problems, you should ask for advice from adults. It will help you find a safe way out. It is also a good opportunity for the auspicious stars "Leng Tek" (Morality Dragon) and "Sam Tai" (Three Sons) to send auspicious energy into the horoscope house to help. It will help encourage and draw your heart back to focus on studying.

Career and Business

This year is a criterion for progress. For students, they still need to be more diligent to have a stable future. Today's diligence will be the foundation for future faculty selection scores. Therefore, it should not be overlooked. If there are any problems, you should consult your parents or teachers to get the best answers.

For working-age people, this year's work is in a good condition. If you set good work goals and cooperate in working together, it will lead to creating greater results that are both beneficial and valuable. Especially during the months when both work and education of the person in both cycles of life will have a good direction of progress and prosperity, namely, the 12th Chinese month (January 5 - February 2), the 3rd Chinese month (April 4 - May 4), the 7th Chinese month (August 7 - September 6), and the 9th Chinese month (October 8 - November 6) for starting something new, joint ventures, and various investments.

This year, you should be careful of problems with capital and accounting fraud, especially during the bad months. Which will cause your work and studies to be obstructed and have problems, including the 2nd Chinese month (March 5 - April 3), the 4th Chinese month (May 5 - June 4), the 5th Chinese month (June 5 - July 6), and the 8th Chinese month (September 7 - October 7). In addition, when signing various contracts, you should look at the details carefully and be careful of shady conditions that will be an obstacle in the future.

Financial

This year is a criterion for progress. For students, they still need to be more diligent to have a stable future. Today's diligence will be the foundation for future faculty selection scores. Therefore, it should not be overlooked. If there are any problems, you should consult your parents or teachers to get the best answers.

For working-age people, this year's work is in a good condition. If you set good work goals and cooperate in working together, it will lead to creating greater results that are both beneficial and valuable. Especially during the months when both work and education of the person in both cycles of life will have a good direction of progress and prosperity, namely, the 12th Chinese month (January 5 - February 2), the 3rd Chinese month (April 4 - May 4), the 7th Chinese month (August 7 - September 6), and the 9th Chinese month (October 8 - November 6) for starting something new, joint ventures, and various investments.

This year, you should be careful of problems with capital and accounting fraud, especially during the bad months. Which will cause your work and studies to be obstructed and have problems, including the 2nd Chinese month (March 5 - April 3), the 4th Chinese month (May 5 - June 4), the 5th Chinese month (June 5 - July 6), and the 8th Chinese month (September 7 - October 7). In addition, when signing various contracts, you should look at the details carefully and be careful of shady conditions that will be an obstacle in the future.

Family

Family events for both horoscopes this year are not very peaceful. This is because the evil star "Xiao Ae" (the planet of danger) is in the horoscope house, which will affect the safety of family members, internal arguments, and minors in the family getting into trouble with neighbors. Problems may escalate to the point of having to move out. In particular, the months when your family will experience chaos are the 2nd Chinese month (March 5 – April 3), the 4th Chinese month (May 5 – June 4), the 5th

Chinese month (June 5 – July 6), and the 8th Chinese month (September 7 – October 7). During this period, in addition to having to check for fasteners in the house that may fall and cause harm, any damaged appliances or electrical appliances should be repaired or replaced immediately to reduce unexpected events. You should also take care of and train your family members to be flexible and lenient, and not to have any problems with anyone to reduce the chances of arguments. In addition, teenage horoscopes should know how to choose their friends. You should avoid hanging out with friends who like to invite you to hang out or engage in vices, and avoid getting involved in conflicts between friends, otherwise, you will be asking for trouble and bring trouble to your family.

Love

For senior horoscopes, this year you should not interfere in other people's family matters, including children. This will make everyone in the house loveable. In particular, when criticizing children, you should not use harsh words. You should use kindness as your main principle.

For teenagers, this year's love criteria is considered good. You will be charming and popular with friends of the opposite sex. Close contact may be promoted from a friend to a close friend. However, love cannot be hasty. Thai teenagers love truly and can wait.

However, you should be careful during the months when love problems will occur, which are the 2nd Chinese month (March 5 - April 3), the 4th Chinese month (May 5 - June 4), the 5th Chinese month (June 5 - July 6), and the 8th Chinese month (September 7 - October 7). Be careful of being deceived or having sweet dreams and assumptions. This will cause problems. Also, you should not interfere in other couples' love affairs because you may be misunderstood as a third party. During the aforementioned months at night, if it is not necessary, please do not go out and hang out. Be careful of something bad happening.

Health

The health of both horoscopes this year is a good sign that hides bad, so you should take care of your health closely. Start with getting enough rest, followed by taking care of your hygiene in terms of eating, both fresh, clean, and nutritious. In particular, you should be careful during the months when your health will have problems, which are the 2nd Chinese month (March 5 - April 3), the 4th Chinese month (May 5 - June 4), the 5th Chinese month (June 5 - July 6), and the 8th Chinese month (September 7 - October 7), when both horoscopes must be more careful of accidents.

For the elderly, be careful of injuries from slipping, falling, or fainting. Be careful of old illnesses acting up and be careful of hidden illnesses that may quietly appear to attack you.

For the young horoscopes, be careful of accidents from playing sports and be careful of going out in groups to party with other groups. There may be conflicts that can lead to dangers to the point of bloodshed.

Year of the Rabbit (Golden | (1963)

" Rabbit in the house" is a person born in the year of the Rabbit at the age of 62 years (1963)

Overview

For the Rabbit year people in this age group, this year, in terms of work and trade, you need to study the details and study carefully before starting, especially projects that require high capital. It would be better if you take this opportunity to move behind the scenes and prepare assistants to help continue the work in the future so that you don't have to be stressed and tired too much. For this year's finances, even though the overall picture looks good because the "Luk Hung Star" (the star of wealth) is orbiting to support you, it is another year that wealth and fortune come to visit. You can choose to invest in various channels to create profits. However, it is important to plan both your manpower and set clear career goals. Always develop new skills to keep up with the world and changes. Because in your horoscope, there are bad stars that are disturbing you. Therefore, you must be careful that there are internal leaks and losses of wealth. There are often unexpected things that cause money to flow out from time to time. You should be careful about health problems, especially the head. Be careful of dizziness. Be careful of high blood pressure and liver disease. In addition, be careful of accidents and unexpected events. When traveling, you should have someone with you. You should take good care of your mental health. You must know how to let go. Don't be stressed about your children because it will affect your physical health.

Career and Business

This year, your career will be smooth. You will find supporters to help you. Therefore, finding an assistant or heir to help continue your work during this time is a good preparation. You will have time to pass on and teach each other for some time. For investment, this year has a bright direction. If you are going to buy stocks, choose a company with a future that is not a speculative stock. Or choose to invest in real gold, not paper. You will receive good returns. The months when your career will flourish are the 12th Chinese month (January 5 - February 2), the 3rd Chinese month (April 4 - May 4), the 7th Chinese month (August 7 - September 6), and the 9th Chinese month (October 8 - November 6). However, this year you should supervise and monitor the signing of employment contracts or hiring yourself because there may be minor details that are overlooked and may cause you to be at a disadvantage later. Also, making other legal contracts should be done carefully and thoroughly. In particular, the months when your work is declining and problems arise include the 2nd Chinese month (5 March - 3 April), the 4th Chinese month (5 May - 4 June), the 5th Chinese month (5 June - 6 July), and the 8th Chinese month (7 September - 7 October). During these times, you should not invest in new things, as there is a possibility of encountering financial embezzlement by your subordinates. Starting a new job and entering into investments will cause many problems.

Financial

This year, your financial horoscope is quite bright. Cash flow will come in from two sources: direct income, such as salary or sales, as well as extra money from special jobs or returns on various investments. This is because you will have the opportunity to expand your career or expand your current business. Furthermore, your investments will have good returns, resulting in increased income. There are several months in which you will have financial luck flowing in: the 12th Chinese Month (January 5 – February 2), the 3rd Chinese Month (April 4 – May 4), the 7th Chinese Month (August 7 – September 6), and the 9th Chinese Month (October 8 – November 6). However, please do not expect money from gambling because you will have more chances of losing than winning. Also, you should not be greedy for fortunes that are not yours. Be careful of falling victim to scammers. The months when your finances will be sluggish and unexpectedly incur expenses are the 2nd Chinese month (March 5 - April 3), the 4th Chinese month (May 5 - June 4), the 5th Chinese month (June 5 - July 6), and the 8th Chinese month (September 7 - October 7). During these months, do not lend money to others or be a guarantor for anyone. Do not gamble and do not invest in businesses that are at risk of being illegal.

Family

Even though this year there are some obstacles, if you diligently go down to check and help solve the problems, the problems that will occur will be just minor ones that will pass. Find time to meet and talk with people in the house, find time to sit around and eat together to discuss, so that you can exchange ideas and receive cooperation in things that are not smooth, helping the house to be peaceful. However, you should be careful during the months when problems and chaos will occur in the family, which are: the 2nd Chinese month (March 5 - April 3), the 4th Chinese month (May 5 - June 4), the 5th Chinese month (June 5 - July 6), the 8th Chinese month (September 7 - October 7) Be careful of juniors in the house having problems with neighbors. Be careful of valuables in the house being damaged, lost, or stolen. Also, do not get involved in conflicts between friends, especially in legal cases.

As for close friends and relatives, it is considered good. If there are obstacles, you will receive help, and help solve some problems that are beyond your ability. There is also an opportunity to open new businesses together.

Love
This year, your love life will be close and intimate. You will have the opportunity to travel with your lover both domestically and internationally. There is a possibility of visiting relatives or attending merit-making ceremonies. The time that has passed with the long journey of love is another period of love that you will remember forever. However, there are some periods when your love will have problems and arguments like the tongue and teeth, such as the 2nd Chinese month (March 5 - April 3), the 4th Chinese month (May 5 - June 4), the 5th Chinese month (June 5 - July 6), and the 8th Chinese month (September 7 -

October 7). You must be careful not to interfere with other people's family problems. In addition, during this period, you should be careful even though you are old. If there is jealousy about service girls, it will be embarrassing to your children and grandchildren. If you make a mistake, you may catch a disease of love. Therefore, you should be firm and know how to conduct yourself.

Health
This year, the health of the person is not very good. You should be careful not to work too hard without resting or not getting enough rest. It will cause you to feel dizzy and faint. You should also be careful of gastritis, intestinal diseases, back pain, osteoarthritis, and hidden diseases. Therefore, when traveling outside, whether by car or boat, walking up and down should be careful because there is a chance of falling and getting injured. The months that you should pay close attention to your health are the 2nd Chinese month (March 5 - April 3), the 4th Chinese month (May 5 - June 4), the 5th Chinese month (June 5 - July 6), and the 8th

Chinese month (September 7 - October 7). During these times, you should be more careful about safety and take care of your food hygiene.

Year of the Rabbit (Wood) | (1975)

" The rabbit has attained enlightenment. " is a person born in the year of the Rabbit at the age of 49 years (1975)

Overview

For those born in the year of the Rabbit, this year is another year in which the zodiac house is filled with auspicious stars, so there is auspicious power to support and encourage you, making your life path in almost every aspect good, whether it is work, finance, love, family, relatives, friends or health. You will have the opportunity to buy expensive property, have the opportunity to expand your business or for those who work regularly, there will be the opportunity to advance to a higher position. This year is therefore suitable for preparing and allocating manpower for a big job. If you have the money and the people, you can start this year. Both internal and external investments will have satisfactory returns. However, during the year, you must be careful of the evil stars "Xiao Er" (the planet of danger) and "Huang Pui" (the star of betrayal) that will come to influence and destroy peace. You should be careful of the causes of words and communication that may cause misunderstandings, causing you to be betrayed by people close to you, causing trouble, damage, and loss of property. Otherwise, there is a chance that you will fall victim to scammers. Therefore, you must be careful and not be careless. In terms of family, this year there will be happy events, auspicious events, or new family members. What you should be careful of this year is your health, which is in menopause and accumulating stress from work, so you cannot neglect it. Because silent diseases may arise and cause problems for you.

Career and Business

This year, both your career and personal business will expand because you will receive supportive power. It will help promote your career to progress. Businesses will flourish, but you may encounter envious people who will obstruct you. This can be solved by improving your human relations skills. Being friendly and sincere to those around you will help you overcome the crisis. The months when your career and investment will have a bright direction are the 12th Chinese month (January 5 - February 2), the 3rd Chinese month (April 4 - May 4), the 7th Chinese month (August 7 - September 6), and the 9th Chinese month (October 8 - November 6), which you will encounter good changes. Therefore, you should prepare your organization, assign people to the right jobs and responsibilities, and set the direction and goals of your career and business well. If everything is ready and the right time comes, you can go all out. As for joint ventures or investments in various fields or buying shares, it is in good condition. You can join the partnership or invest in the stock market. It is expected that at the end of the year, you will receive dividends or the value of the shares will increase.

However, be careful when signing contracts to conduct legal transactions. Be careful not to be deceived. In particular, the months when work will change for the worse and encounter problems are the 2nd Chinese month (March 5 - April 3), the 4th Chinese month (May 5 - June 4), the 5th Chinese month (June 5 - July 6), and the 8th Chinese month (September 7 - October 7). You should not invest or enter into partnerships with anyone to do business. You should also be careful of insiders acting as spies for your competitors or making damaging mistakes but not being able to catch them.

Financial

This year is a year of abundant income. Cash flow will flow in two ways, directly from your regular salary or income from sales of goods or services, as well as special income such as brokerage fees, and bonuses, including money from luck and investments in various areas. This year is quite bright. If you choose to buy the right thing at the right time and release it at the right time, you have the right to be rich. Also, investing in expanding your own business is quite smooth. In particular, the months when your finances will flow smoothly are the 12th Chinese month (January 5 – February 2), the 3rd Chinese month (April 4 – May 4), the 7th Chinese month (August 7 – September 6), and the 9th Chinese month (October 8 – November 6). However, you should be careful during the months when your financial luck will decline and you may experience financial difficulties, such as the 2nd Chinese month (March 5 – April 3), the 4th Chinese month (May 5 – June 4), the 5th Chinese month (June 5 – July 6), and the 8th Chinese month (September 7 – October 7). During these periods, you must not lend money to others, sign financial guarantees, or gamble. Furthermore, you must not get involved in illegal businesses or copyright infringement.

Family

This year, the family horoscope will receive auspicious power to support, which will promote auspicious work in the house. There will be an opportunity to add new members to the house. There will be an auspicious time to move into a new house. You will meet a patron.

In addition, you will find support and help from friends. Help each other solve crises and overcome them together. However, you should be careful during the low months as there will be conflicts and chaos in your family, such as the 2nd Chinese month (March 5 - April 3), the 4th Chinese month (May 5 - June 4), the 5th Chinese month (June 5 - July 6), and the 8th Chinese month (September 7 - October 7). Be careful of some friends who will betray you and do not get involved in the conflicts of friends. In addition, be careful of safety in the house. Be careful of valuables being damaged or dangers from unexpected criminals.

Love

This year, your love life is quite smooth. You will have the opportunity to take your lover to visit distant relatives or go on a trip together. It is also a good time for parents to help plan for their children to marry and create a new family institution. Both welcoming a daughter-in-law or marrying a daughter should consult each other. There is only the period of the 2nd Chinese month (March 5 - April 3), the 4th

Chinese month (May 5 - June 4), the 5th Chinese month (June 5 - July 6), and the 8th Chinese month (September 7 - October 7) that the power of the peach blossom enters the house. You will be charming and the opposite sex will be interested in you. However, you should understand the monogamous system. No partner will share their lover with someone else. Therefore, being charming is a good thing, but don't forget to think about the other person's feelings. Therefore, you should avoid interfering in other people's family matters and avoid going to entertainment venues that will bring arguments and illnesses.

Health

This year, the health of the person at the beginning of the year is good, but after the middle of the year, there is a chance of getting sick, so you should be careful of stomach diseases, intestinal diseases, high blood pressure, headaches, migraines or food poisoning, especially during the 2nd Chinese month (March 5 - April 3), 4th Chinese month (May 5 - June 4), 5th Chinese month (June 5 -

July 6), 8th Chinese month (September 7 - October 7) when you should be careful of the exacerbation of these diseases. You should also be careful of accidents during work and travel due to insufficient rest. You should also avoid cold-element foods and cold-natured foods.

Year of the Rabbit (Fire) | (1987)
" The Rabbit at the Full Moon" is a person born in the year of the Rabbit at the age of 38 years (1987)

Overview
For those born in the year of the Rabbit, this year is another year that your work and business must be patient and diligent to achieve success and progress. Although there are auspicious stars to help, the money that you will receive this year depends on your diligence in earning a living and constantly developing new skills that are up to date with the situation. The more you do, the more you will get. You should also work and save so that you can accumulate a large sum of money that can be

invested or used for other benefits. Because in the horoscope, there is an evil star, "Xiao Ae" (a planet of danger), causing trouble. Therefore, this is another year that every step you take forward must be careful. Do not be hasty. When accepting or giving orders, you must communicate clearly to prevent mistakes from occurring. In the implementation of various tasks, there will be problems, obstacles, and accidents both during work and travel. Especially if you attend a party where alcohol is consumed, you should avoid driving or working with machinery. Also, be careful of arguing about trivial matters with people close to you. However, during the year, auspicious stars will orbit to help reduce disasters. Therefore, the horoscope owner should use the smooth period to work hard to create results and increase sales to save money for times when the time is not good. In terms of relatives and friends, this year you should choose people to be friends with. Because your fate this year will be to meet friends who like to flatter and persuade you in a bad way, you must know how to behave and reject people. You should avoid going out, drinking alcohol, and going to entertainment venues.

Career and Business

This year, your work will encounter obstacles and storms. You will be challenged. To earn money, you will have to use every strategy and method to get it, and it will not be easy. You will have to go through many battles and fights along the way. In addition, you should be careful of conflicts in your department and misunderstandings with customers or those you have to contact. In addition, those who work regularly should be careful of having problems with relationships with both their superiors and subordinates continuously. Especially during the months when your work will be stuck and have many obstacles, such as the 2nd Chinese month (March 5 - April 3), the 4th Chinese month (May 5 - June 4), the 5th Chinese month (June 5 - July 6), and the 8th Chinese month (September 7 - October 7). During these times, you should be patient and manage your relationships well. When signing any legal contracts, be careful not to be at a disadvantage. In addition, avoid investing because it may lead to a lack of liquidity in your capital. Be careful of subordinates causing problems or being cheated by your partners. The impact of the external economic crisis will also cause your business to suffer. However, there are many periods when starting a new job, investing in joint ventures, and investing in various areas will yield good returns, including the 12th Chinese Month (January 5 – February 2), the 3rd Chinese Month (April 4 – May 4), the 7th Chinese Month (August 7 – September 6), and the 9th Chinese Month (October 8 – November 6).

Financial

This year, the fortune of the person is not smooth. Income and expenses seem to be close together. It is not easy to earn money. You should be careful in investing. Plan carefully and research the market well. Do not be greedy for a little bit of money that will cause you to lose a lot of money and cause trouble. Especially in the months that are not favorable to you, which are the 2nd Chinese month

(March 5 - April 3), the 4th Chinese month (May 5 - June 4), the 5th Chinese month (June 5 - July 6), and the 8th Chinese month (September 7 - October 7). Do not lend money to others or guarantee anyone. Do not gamble. Do not invest in businesses that are likely to be against the law. Do not be greedy for wealth that does not belong to you because it will be the cause of losing capital and coming back to hurt yourself. The months when your finances will be liquid are the 12th Chinese month (5 January – 2 February), the 3rd Chinese month (4 April – 4 May), the 7th Chinese month (7 August – 6 September), and the 9th Chinese month (8 October – 6 November).

Family

This year, there will be a mix of bad and good things in the house. This is because the horoscope house has a bad star pointing at the family horoscope. Therefore, the person of the horoscope must be more careful because there is a chance that unexpected events will occur in the house. There will be health problems with family members, especially in the months that are not conducive to you and internal conflicts will easily arise, such as the 2nd Chinese month (March 5 - April 3), the 4th Chinese month (May 5 - June 4), the 5th Chinese month (June 5 - July 6), and the 8th Chinese month (September 7 - October 7). During these times, be careful of accidents in the house that may result in bloodshed. Also, be careful of valuables being damaged, lost, or stolen. For relatives and friends, this year is good. They will receive support and help solve some problems that occur so that they can be overcome smoothly. However, be careful of talking carelessly as it may cause misunderstandings. Therefore, you should only talk about the truth and necessity. This will help reduce the chances of making offensive remarks that may cause disagreements without realizing it.

Love

This year, your love life is not smooth. Part of it is your mood that is easily irritated and your inconsistency, which causes you to argue back and forth. Sometimes you can't control your emotions and explode at the other person, which often leads to arguments. Sometimes, there will be problems with jealousy or misunderstandings due to a third party or from the instigation of ill-wishers, which leads to serious arguments. You must remember that to be a couple, in addition to having love, you must also be honest and trust each other. Don't be easily influenced by ill-wishers. Before expecting the other person to change, it would be better to start by improving yourself first. Therefore, if you hope for your love to last, you will have to let go of your stubbornness, face an understanding, and forgive each other. In particular, the months when love is fragile and things can easily cause frustration and irritation are the 2nd Chinese month (5 March - 3 April), the 4th Chinese month (5 May - 4 June), the 5th Chinese month (5 June - 6 July), and the 8th Chinese month (7 September - 7 October). You should avoid going to entertainment venues that sell services.

Health

This year, the health of this person is not good. They often have frequent headaches, are easily allergic to the weather, feel exhausted, have undesirable feelings, and sometimes have heartaches and insomnia. This kind of illness must be solved by starting with yourself, who must let go. Find free time to do activities that help relieve stress and fatigue. Or maybe go play sports to exercise, which will help strengthen your body and mind. However, you should be careful during the months when your health will have complications, which are: the 2nd Chinese month (March 5 - April 3), the 4th Chinese month (May 5 - June 4), the 5th Chinese month (June 5 - July 6), the 8th Chinese month (September 7 - October 7). During these times, if you find anything unusual in your body, you should see a doctor for treatment. Do not ignore it for too long, it will be dangerous. You should also be more careful both while working and traveling. Do not be careless about your safety.

Chinese Astrology Horoscope for Each Month

Month 12 in the Dragon Year (5 Jan 25 - 2 Feb 25)

The life path of those born in the year of the Rabbit, this month has a bright and prosperous direction because whether it is business or work, you will find a patron to promote you to progress.

Therefore, you should use this opportunity to publicize your work and business to make it known. You should also plan your work, allocate a budget for operations, and wait for the right time to start working until you achieve your goals. The important thing during this period is that when the water rises, you should scoop it up quickly and push forward the projects that you have planned to take shape and progress.

However, you should be careful that whoever has a long hand may snatch it first. Therefore, when the opportunity and timing are open, it would be a pity if you do not seize it. This month is an opportunity to expand, gain profits, or create more work. You can also start a new job or invest in a partnership this month. You will see beautiful returns. Finances are moderate. During this period, even though you have new ways to expand your income, if you spend lavishly or invest carelessly without planning and being careful, it may cause your money to be liquid. Therefore, you must plan your spending well from the beginning of the year so that you will not have problems with being in the red later. This month, you will mostly meet good friends who will help you and give you useful advice to use in your work or business.

Family is peaceful. Obstructed and having problems, still receiving kindness from elders

As for love, this period is fresh and bright like a fish in the water because there is a chance that there will be someone of the opposite sex who is interested and close, always helping and caring. If you don't think about it yet, such as your lover wanting to be friends, you will have a good friendship.

As for health, even if you find a minor illness, it is still considered normal. But if you have time, you should take care of your health to be stronger than before so that you will have energy for new work that comes in.

Support Days: 2 Jan., 6 Jan., 10 Jan., 14 Jan., 18 Jan., 22 Jan., 26 Jan., 30 Jan.
Lucky Days: 5 Jan., 17 Jan., 29 Jan.
Misfortune Days: 4 Jan., 16 Jan., 28 Jan.
Bad Days: 1 Jan., 11 Jan., 13 Jan., 23 Jan., 25 Jan.

Month 1 in the Snake Year (3 Feb 25 - 4 Mar 25)
This month, the horoscope of those born in the year of the Rabbit still receives supportive power from the auspicious stars that continue to shine. Therefore, the horoscope graph has the power to soar forward. Your career and business are well-received and are on the rise. Various problems that have accumulated from work are starting to ease and ease. What you should do on this occasion is to always create and strengthen good relationships in your work line, both at the top and bottom levels, including business partners, customers, and those you always contact, to wait for a good

opportunity to start a big project. This is considered to be the important foundation of a tall building. This month, your finances will have good income and cash flow, but you should save it for a period of obstacles and stagnation so that you will not be left with a dry face.

The family is peaceful. During this period, there is a chance to organize an auspicious event. There is an auspicious time to move into a new house or change your workplace. Otherwise, you may receive good news about the success of your family members. Regarding close relatives and friends, this period is good. You will meet good friends who will give you advice and may spark something that will help increase your work or expand your business. This will help your work and business progress even more. Starting a new job, investing in shares, and investing in various channels are good opportunities during this period. Suitable for increasing investment, expanding work, will have good returns.

In terms of sweet love, it is a time when flowers bloom and honey is sweet. For some couples, love is ripe and they want to settle down. Therefore, if you are sure about the other person and are ready, you can find an auspicious time to spend your life together in the future during this period.

In terms of health, you will see a good doctor with good medicine. Even if you are sick, there is nothing to worry about. However, you should get enough rest and take care of your food and drink cleanliness.

Support Days: 3 Feb., 7 Feb., 11 Feb., 15 Feb., 19 Feb., 23 Feb., 27 Feb.
Lucky Days: 10 Feb., 22 Feb.
Misfortune Days: 9 Feb., 21 Feb.
Bad Days: 4 Feb., 6 Feb., 16 Feb., 18 Feb., 28 Feb.

Month 2 in the Snake Year (5 Mar 25 - 3 Apr 25)

This month, your horoscope is stuck, so the road of life is rough, causing you to face challenging career tests and still encounter conflicts that have not been resolved. What you should do during this period is to do your best and learn to use your potential. Encourage yourself, set goals, and reach them. Also, be diligent and patient, and ask for advice from elders. In addition, you must check your internal information to prevent corruption and money leakage.

This month, your finances are in a state of losing money, with little income and many expenses. Also, be careful of unexpected expenses. Therefore, please avoid gambling and taking risks. Do not do businesses that are at risk of violating the law because you may encounter legal problems and lose your money. Also, do not be greedy for the profits that others deceive you. Be careful of falling victim to scammers.

For work, you still need to be careful, both in business negotiations and contract documents. Be careful of being cheated. Working together or thinking of investing in anything during this period should wait for now.

For family, be careful of family members who may have accidents that cause bloodshed. Also, be careful of juniors causing trouble.

In terms of love, it is in the middle range. Even though during this period, there are often disagreements or disagreements, we can still talk about it. But you should avoid going to entertainment venues because you may encounter dangers.

In terms of health, during this period, be careful of diseases that come through the mouth, including other infectious diseases. You should also be careful of accidents while traveling.

Support Days: 3 Mar., 7 Mar., 11 Mar., 15 Mar., 19 Mar., 23 Mar., 27Mar., 31 Mar.
Lucky Days: 6 Mar., 18 Mar., 30 Mar.

Misfortune Days: 5 Mar., 17 Mar., 29 Mar.
Bad Days: 2 Mar., 12 Mar., 14 Mar., 24 Mar., 26 Mar.

Month 3 in the Snake Year (4 Apr 25 - 4 May 25)
This month, the life path of those born in the year of the Rabbit is bright and shining, causing the direction of the horoscope to soar. In terms of work and business, it will be bright and lively again. Therefore, you should prepare for work or investment in various channels. Turn the crisis into an opportunity. For obstacles that are stuck because the boss or supervisor doesn't like you, and subordinates tend not to cooperate, this month you will meet an elder who helps to resolve and help your work go smoothly. However, you must be careful about your words and always think before you speak. You should also not interfere or interfere in other people's matters because you risk getting caught up in the net and causing trouble.

As for the fortune and finances, this period is quite good because we have come across a supportive month, resulting in continuous cash flow, both direct income from salary or sales, as well as special money from special work and windfall luck. However, since this month there will be an unexpected outflow of funds, you should manage with caution.

For the family, this month is peaceful and there may be special guests visiting the house during this period.

Your health is quite good. As for your love life, this is another period when you are full of charm. There will be people of the opposite sex who will come close to you and take care of you. There will also be an opportunity to meet friends of the opposite sex who understand you and have the opportunity to develop a relationship from friends to lovers.

Support Days: 4 Apr., 8 Apr., 12 Apr., 16 Apr., 20 Apr., 24 Apr., 28 Apr.
Lucky Days: 11 Apr., 23 Apr.
Misfortune Days: 10 Apr., 22 Apr.

Bad Days: 5 Apr., 7 Apr., 17 Apr., 19 Apr., 29 Apr.

Month 4 in the Snake Year (5 May 25 - 4 Jun 25)
This month, for the Rabbit, the situation is still in a gloomy and unsmooth state. The important thing to be careful of is the liquidity problem of working capital, work, or business that shows signs of conflict and the unexpected. In terms of work and business, there will be chaos due to conflicts among people in the organization. Be careful that it will affect and cause big work to go wrong or be damaged. In addition, during this time, you must be careful about communication, whether it is about hiring or hiring or making contracts because it will bring damage. Therefore, what the Rabbit should do on this occasion is to be patient and calm, and build and maintain good relationships with people around you at all times, so that the problem does not worsen.

This month, your financial luck is in the position of losing money. Be careful of account leakage points for those who do business. And be careful of unexpected current expenses that will interfere and cause you to lack liquidity. Therefore, this month, you should stay away from investing in windfalls, both gambling, stocks, or gold, including investing in risky businesses. You must be strict with yourself in saving, tightening your belt, and managing your spending to be balanced.

However, for matters within the family, there is peace and harmony. If there are any obstacles or problems, During this time, turn to your home to receive help. As for love, if one of you is willing to back down and reduce arguing, it will certainly help reduce the quarrels that often annoy you. Health still needs care and attention. During this time, be careful that not getting enough rest will cause you to fall ill, get food poisoning, and get slightly sick depending on the weather. You should avoid drinking alcohol, which can be harmful to others and yourself.

Support Days: 2 May, 6 May, 10 May, 14 May, 18 May, 22 May, 26 May, 30 May.
Lucky Days: 5 May, 17 May, 29 May.
Misfortune Days: 4 May, 16 May, 28 May.
Bad Days: 1 May, 11 May, 13 May, 23 May, 25 May.

Month 5 in the Snake Year (5 Jun 25 - 6 Jul 25)
This month, your horoscope has a bad star orbiting and harassing you, causing your horoscope to fall out of the normal line. Your career and business are therefore beset with old and new problems and obstacles. Therefore, what you should do this month is to speak less and work more. Also, try to be careful and avoid problems with people around you because there is a chance that people will be jealous, slander and find ways to bully you. In addition, the influence of the bad star will cause you to have a violent temper and be easily irritated, which will cause small problems to escalate into big problems. Therefore, you should control your temper. When doing any activity, you should keep your

cool. Being hasty will only bring about greater dangers.

Your financial horoscope this month is not good because there will be only things that will pull money out of your pocket. You must closely monitor your accounts to prevent corruption. Also, valuables should be kept safe. Beware of scammers. You should also avoid gambling and taking chances on unexpected windfalls. Do not invest in immoral or illegal businesses because there is a chance of being sued for legal actions.

Your work is in a monsoon. Be careful when making contacts and conducting legal contracts. You must be careful with the details. Beware of being cheated and taken advantage of. This month is not good for investment.

Your family will lack peace. There is a possibility of health and safety problems in the family, causing you to be restless.

In terms of love, you will encounter disagreements and arguments due to a third party. However, during this period, you should not escape to entertainment venues because it will be like pouring oil on the fire and making the problem worse.

In terms of health, during this period, be careful of accidents that may cause you injury.

Support Days: 3 Jun., 7 Jun., 11 Jun., 15 Jun., 19 Jun., 23 Jun., 27 Jun.
Lucky Days: 10 Jun., 22 Jun.
Misfortune Days: 9 Jun., 21 Jun.
Bad Days: 4 Jun., 6 Jun., 16 Jun., 18 Jun., 28 Jun., 30 Jun.

Month 6 in the Snake Year (7 Jul 25 - 6 Aug 25)
Your destiny this month is fluctuating and unstable, causing many good opportunities that might come to your hand to be snatched away by others first. Coupled with your mind during this period, it is often unstable and uncertain and you are still not brave enough to make a decision, causing your work to stumble and have problems. In terms of work and

business, during this period, you still need to use your wits more because if you act slowly, you may miss out, but if you rush and make a mistake, it will be bad. You should be more careful. When you have made a plan, you should have both a plan B and a plan D to prevent mistakes and damages. In addition, what you should do this month is to take care of your work and duties as best you can. Avoid interfering in other people's matters. Before starting any work, study, analyze, and plan thoroughly before doing it. Do not make decisions in favor of yourself, as this will cause you to get hurt later.

For moderate financial destiny, cash flow from salary or sales will continue to flow in. However, you should not gamble because it will affect your existing liquidity and may create long-term debt that you cannot fully repay. During this period, you must be careful and not trust anyone. You must trust half and be careful half to be safe. Collaboration and investment are not good.

For your family's destiny, there is still a hidden disaster. In particular, what should not be neglected is the health of the elderly in the house. In addition, you should regularly check things that are fixed in the house, including equipment, tools, and electrical appliances that are old or damaged. You should find a way to repair or replace them to prevent unexpected incidents for family members.

In terms of love, it is still a smooth time. The tree of love is blooming and bearing fruit. You are in love.

The health horoscope is moderate. You will catch a cold, have allergies, be careful of food poisoning, and be careful of accidents while traveling. Regarding relatives,

Support Days: 1 Jul., 5 Jul., 9 Jul., 13 Jul., 17 Jul., 21 Jul., 25 Jul., 29 Jul.
Lucky Days: 4 Jul., 16 Jul., 28 Jul.
Misfortune Days: 3 Jul., 15 Jul., 27 Jul.
Bad Days: 10 Jul., 12 Jul., 22 Jul., 24 Jul.

Month 7 in the Snake Year (7 Aug 25 - 6 Sep 25)
This month, those born in the year of the Rabbit will receive auspicious power from the auspicious stars that will shine again. The auspicious power will influence to help your career progress and your business flourish. You will also find new paths or opportunities in terms of making a living. Therefore, you should be diligent and determined to move forward and seize opportunities. Do not let the good things that come in during this period pass you by without doing anything to make them grow into something significant. Your salary will be quite good this month. Cash flow will flow in from many sources. You will also be able to reap the rewards from what you are currently doing and what you have invested in before. However, if you are going to take risks or invest in windfalls, you should be careful and not be greedy. If you get it, you must know when to stop. If you have planned your finances before, even if you are feeling dizzy, you will be able to get through this period without much difficulty.

As for investment in various matters during this period, you still need to have a plan for two or three. In terms of work and trade, during this period, because you will find someone to help you, it is a good opportunity to create work, make sales, and expand your income. Therefore, you should increase your diligence and constantly improve your skills to save money.

In terms of your family, you will be peaceful and smooth. You will receive advice on how to improve your work and expand your business. It is a good opportunity to help promote progress.

But in terms of love, it will be a period when both of you have urgent business to attend to, causing you to have no time for each other. Therefore, you should set aside time to be close to each other to add sweetness and strengthen your relationship. Avoid listening to criticism and gossip that does not create any benefit in your relationship. Then everything will be fine.

In terms of health, there will be no bad things to bother you.

Support Days: 2 Aug., 6 Aug., 10 Aug., 14 Aug., 18 Aug., 22 Aug., 26 Aug., 30 Aug.
Lucky Days: 9 Aug., 21 Aug.
Misfortune Days: 8 Aug., 20 Aug.
Bad Days: 3 Aug., 5 Aug., 15 Aug., 17 Aug., 27 Aug., 29 Aug.

Month 8 in the Snake Year (7 Sep 25 - 7 Oct 25)
This month, your horoscope is in the conflict energy line, which will cause conflicts and unexpected events in your work and business. Be careful of confusion in your work dealings, which will lead to mistakes and damages. Legal contracts are another period where you need to be careful of hidden details that put you at a disadvantage. What you should do on this occasion is not to interfere with other people's duties and not to dig up old issues. Maintain humility towards your superiors and subordinates, as well as the people you have to deal with. Hold on to sincerity and honesty. In

addition, please always remember to do good but do not stand out because it will be dangerous. Do not be at the forefront of matters that are not your business. This month, your finances will be in a state of losing money. You should not gamble, take risks, or lend money to anyone. Do not do copyright infringement or be involved in illegal activities. Working together and investing this month is not good. You should postpone it for now.

In terms of family, there is a chance of conflict and arguments within the home. Be careful of servants causing trouble.

In terms of love this month, you need to be careful with your words. Do not be charming or too close to the opposite sex, which will cause misunderstanding among your family members. This will be the cause of rifts. In addition, during this period, there may be disagreements, leading to arguments. Therefore, you should avoid prolonging things. Health is not good. Beware of stomach diseases, liver diseases, and various infectious diseases that will threaten you. In addition, insufficient rest and accumulated stress will cause illnesses. You should also be careful of unexpected accidents.

Support Days: 4 Sep., 8 Sep., 12 Sep., 16 Sep., 20 Sep., 25 Sep., 28 Sep.
Lucky Days: 7 Sep, 20 Sep.
Misfortune Days: 7 Sep, 20 Sep.
Bad Days: 6 Sep, 19 Sep, 30 Sep.

Month 9 in the Snake Year (8 Oct 25 - 6 Nov 25)
This month, your horoscope has the auspicious power to support you, which will help your life path change for the better. Problems will find supporters. This period is another period when you can think and do any work and it will be successful according to your goals. Therefore, what you should do this month is to improve and correct your shortcomings. You should be patient with conflicts to help your work go smoothly.

Your finances this month are moderate. Direct income is good, but be careful not to be greedy because you will lose more than you gain. Therefore, please be diligent in earning money from direct work. You will have a beautiful income flowing in.

In terms of work, since you have someone to help as a consultant, you will have the opportunity to improve your old work and create new work. Various operations that were previously stuck will start to flow more smoothly. During this period, you should prepare everything. When everything is in order, you will get the green light and can move forward with various projects. As for starting a new job, joint ventures, and investments, this period still has good opportunities.

In terms of family horoscope, be careful of family members getting injured in accidents. Be careful of losing property from subordinates or thieves breaking into your home.

In terms of love, be careful of using your emotions. You should control your behavior and control your emotions well. Because if you make one mistake, you may be distrusted forever.

Health horoscope: Be careful of accidents that may cause you to be injured or bleed, especially after a party. If you drink alcohol, do not drive.

Support Days: 1 Oct., 5 Oct., 9 Oct., 13 Oct., 17 Oct., 21 Oct., 25 Oct., 29 Oct.
Lucky Days: 8 Oct., 20 Oct.
Misfortune Days: 7 Oct., 19 Oct., 31 Oct.
Bad Days: 2 Oct., 4 Oct., 14 Oct., 16 Oct., 26 Oct., 28 Oct.

Month 10 in the Snake Year (7 Nov 25 - 6 Dec 25)
This month, the horoscope of those born in the year of the Rabbit is considered a time when the sky is clear, helping the overall picture to be prosperous and flourishing. Your career and business will show progress. Therefore, you should not be indifferent but must be diligent

in your work by constantly creating results, expanding sales and income, and moving forward to seize opportunities. If you let time pass, you will regretfully miss out on good opportunities. What you should do this month is to take the prepared plans and continuously push them forward so that the work becomes tangible and clear and achieves the goals. In addition, you should use this month to solve various problems that are obstacles and pending problems and may ask for cooperation from related partners to prepare for new changes that are coming. Because in terms of work, during this period, there will be some internal improvements to make things better. In addition, there will be a lot of support for you. Therefore, you should use this opportunity to clear up old problems while improving and developing new work to make it progress. The more diligent you are, the more chances you will have to earn money. As for starting a new job, joint ventures, and various investments, this period is still smooth.

This month, your financial fortune will be flowing in. You can invest according to your plan.

For families, this month, there will be good news about auspicious work in the house. There may be new family members. Or you have a chance to move into a new house. As for love, for those who have prepared in advance, this month is a good sign because you have a good time for asking for a proposal, getting engaged, getting married, or moving out. Therefore, it is a good time for two people to come and live together as a couple and build a family institution together.

In terms of health, the body is strong.

Support Days: 2 Nov., 6 Nov., 10 Nov., 14 Nov., 18 Nov., 22 Nov., 26 Nov., 30 Nov.
Lucky Days: 1 Nov., 13 Nov., 25 Nov.
Misfortune Days: 12 Nov., 24 Nov.
Bad Days: 7 Nov., 9 Nov., 19 Nov., 21 Nov.

Month 11 in the Snake Year (7 Dec 25 - 4 Jan 26)
The fate of those born in the year of the Rabbit is entering the last month of the year because it falls into the destroyer line. The fate is therefore unstable. Whether to move forward or backward is difficult. Also, your mind is quite confused during this period.

Although your career and business are full of obstacles and problems, many things depend on your management. If you know how to place the right people in the right jobs, it will help reduce mistakes a lot. In addition, you must know how to assess your potential. Do not be too greedy. Because if you accept a job and cannot do it, or do not manage your time well, you may have to pay a fine and damage your reputation. What you should do this month is to dare to do and accept it. You should dare to listen to criticism, blame, mistakes, or things that are not right. You should also promise to fix them correctly. If you can do it, you will receive help from people around you as before. This month, your finances will encounter storms. There will be many unexpected expenses. As a result, you may experience a financial crisis. Therefore, you should spend thriftily, reduce your luxuries, and not earn money by taking risks with illegal businesses. In addition, you should not gamble or speculate. As for joint ventures and various investments, be careful of sweet-talkers who create fake images and deceive you into losing your money.

During this period, your family should be careful of arguments in the home. And be careful of becoming a victim of fraud. Relatives and friends are still in the criteria of visiting each other normally. Not very good but not causing you any trouble.

Overall, your health is quite good, but you still have to adhere to the principle of not being careless at all times.
Exercise regularly.

In terms of love, even though it is in the middle criteria, you should behave well. If you don't understand each other, please accept it. Try to take care of your heart. Avoid going to entertainment venues. Everyone who loves each other wants the other person to take care of them. Therefore, it is best to avoid the cause of arguments.

Support Days: 4 Dec., 8 Dec., 12 Dec., 16 Dec., 20 Dec., 24 Dec., 28 Dec.
Lucky Days: 7 Dec., 19 Dec., 31 Dec.
Misfortune Days: 6 Dec., 18 Dec., 30 Dec.
Bad Days: 1 Dec., 3 Dec., 13 Dec., 15 Dec., 25 Dec., 27 Dec.

Amulet for The Year of the Rabbit

"Guan Yu bestows wealth and power."
Those born in the year of the Rabbit this year should set up and worship the sacred object "God Guan Yu bestows wealth and power" to enhance their destiny. Place it on your work desk or cash desk to ask for his power and authority to help eliminate disasters, help bring wealth and money to flow in abundance, and help enhance the destiny and family to be peaceful and happy, and for career and business to progress and flourish.

In one chapter of the Advanced Feng Shui, it was mentioned that the deity who will descend to reside in the Mie Keng (house of destiny) of the year is a deity who can bring both good and bad things to the deity of that year. Therefore, worshiping to enhance your destiny with a deity who descends to reside in the same year as your birth year is considered to have the best results and have the most impact on you. This is to rely on the power of that deity to help protect you while your destiny is declining and having bad luck to alleviate it. At the same time, ask for his blessing to help inspire your business and business to be smooth and as desired, and bring glory and prosperity to you and your family.

Those born in the year of the Rabbit or Mie Keng (the horoscope house) in the zodiac sign of the Bao, your overall horoscope this year is quite smooth. Because you are influenced by auspicious stars, helping your business and career to flourish and progress. But you have to be more patient and diligent. Your efforts will be successful. As for various investments, they will give good returns. And you will receive support from your elders. But because there are inauspicious stars in your horoscope that are harassing you, this year there are hidden dangers. Therefore, you cannot trust anyone easily. In April and May, be careful of people close to you who may turn into ill-wishers. Be careful of envious people who will harm or harm you.

You also have to be careful of scammers. In terms of finances, there will be unexpected losses of money and you may also have to get involved in conflicts with others. Traveling both near and far this year, be careful of accidents. In terms of love, there is a possibility. But with a rather stubborn personality, it seems that your love will not come together. Health is quite good. But be careful of the flu and migraines. If you want to solve or alleviate the disaster, you should set up and worship "God Guan Yu bestows wealth and power" to request his power and prestige to help protect you from all kinds of disasters and dangers, and to help the owner of the horoscope live in peace and happiness, create more auspicious wealth and assets, and promote business and trade to be smooth and progressive, and be filled with fortune and luck throughout the year. God Guan Yu is a person who keeps his word in his life, loves virtue, is honest, and is loyal to those who have done him favors all his life. His weapon is an "82-chang halberd", a skilled warhorse named "Chek Tao", and he has two favorite warlords, "Guan Ping" and "Zhou Chong". The Chinese and Thai people respect him as the god of honesty and justice, protecting him from evil and dangers, and bringing fortune and prosperity to the home and family. He is also the god of victory (victory in a hundred battles), therefore it helps to enhance the power and prestige in governance, making wicked people retreat. The followers are obedient and help enhance wealth and prosperity. Worshiping "God Guan Yu bestows wealth and power" is suitable for those born in the year of the Rabbit who are in business because it means a quick and agile response in a critical situation. It also helps to enhance good fortune and auspicious things.

In addition, those born in the year of the Rabbit should wear a lucky pendant of "God Guan Yu bestows wealth and power" around their necks or carry it with them when traveling outside the home, both near and far, so that the person will be filled with wealth and auspicious places, have prosperity and progress in both business and trade and have a peaceful and happy family throughout the year, resulting in better and faster efficiency and effectiveness than before.

Good Direction: Northwest, Southwest, and East
Bad Direction: West
Lucky Colors: Green, Light Blue, Black, Gray, and Blue.
Lucky Times: 05.00 – 06.59, 13.00 – 14.59, 19.00 – 21.59.
Bad Times: 07.00 – 08.59, 11.00 – 11.59, 17.00 – 18.59.

Good Luck For 2025